ABOUT PRINC

by

Trevor James

ORCHARD PUBLICATIONS
2   Orchard Close, Chudleigh, Newton Abbot, Devon TQ13 0LR
Telephone: (01626) 852714

Copyright © Trevor James 2002

ISBN 1 898964 74 5

Printed by:
Hedgerow Print, Crediton, Devon EX17 1ES

ABOUT PRINCETOWN

Sir Thomas Tyrwhitt

Photo courtesy of Paul Rendell
(reproduced by permission of
the Governing Body,
Christchurch, Oxford)

Princetown was founded by Sir Thomas Tyrwhitt, an influential and wealthy gentleman who came to Dartmoor in 1785. He built a country home, Tor Royal, on what was then open moorland and set his heart on creating an agricultural community there. Among the posts he held were:

1795   Private Secretary to the Prince of Wales.
1796   Secretary and Auditor to the Duchy of Cornwall.
1803   Lord Warden of the Stannaries.
1812   Knighted and made Usher of Black Rod.

He had also served as Member of Parliament for Okehampton, Portarlington, and Plymouth.

Tor Royal as it is today. Photo courtesy of Paul Rendell

Princetown – the name

It began with the construction of a road in 1772 from Tavistock to Moretonhampstead which opened up the remote parts of the moor and attracted well-off developers. The nucleus around which they congregated was the Two Bridges area, so named because there were then two bridges, one over the River Cowsic and another across the East Dart river. This district was known as 'Prince Town' years before Sir Thomas Tyrwhitt arrived, which suggests the name was adopted by him to include the new town he founded and as a tribute to his friend the Prince of Wales, the future King George 4th.

Two Bridges – a romantic view from the past. The Ashburton road with the turning left to Moretonhampstead can be seen above and to the right of the settlement.

The Mast

The first thing every visitor sees on the approach to Princetown is the 700ft. high B.B.C. radio mast which surmounts North Hessary Tor. It was originally installed to transmit TV programmes, the first of which was sent out in August 1956 three years after construction work began. Today television is beamed to Princetown only, the mast's prime purpose being the transmission of radio programmes over an area embracing the whole of Devon and parts of Dorset and Cornwall as well, ranging from Bridport in the east to Truro in the west. Signals received from Broadcasting House are decoded and amplified before transmission. It is one of several such stations around the country and the staff service sites west of Exeter as far as the Scilly Isles.

The BBC radio mast on Hessary Tor dominates Princetown.

The mast is constructed of steel girders, weighs 250 tons and is supported by several thick steel wire stays. The base is an inverted apex mounted on a four inch (approx. 10cm) diameter ball bearing which permits limited movement in the almost constant winds that gust from the Channel to the crest of the tor. The top of the mast oscillates about 2ft under the worst conditions. Periodic checks entail a vertical climb of an hour up a steel ladder within the framework (for maintenance work tools and replacement parts are taken up by an external hoist). Winters here are more severe than perhaps anywhere on the moor. In the late 1970s the staff were marooned in deep snow for three days, living on Mars bars and crisps, without electricity and the water supply frozen. On one occasion a chunk of ice as big as a dustbin broke from the mast and embedded itself in the switchroom roof.

The Town Centre.
If you look out from the steps of the High Moorland Visitor Centre the Plume of Feathers inn is to your right. It is the oldest building in Princetown and was built by Sir Thomas Tyrwhitt to provide shelter for the workers he employed until suitable housing could be made available for them. The name of the inn is a reference to the Coat of Arms of the Prince of Wales which has as its crest 'three silver or white feathers rising through a gold coronet of alternate crosses and fleur-de-lys' with the words 'Ich Dien' (I Serve) underneath.

The Visitor Centre building dates from when Dartmoor prison was built (1806–1809) to provide living quarters for the officers of the Army and Militia forces who guarded the French and American prisoners of war. Princetown soon developed as a busy garrison town with hundreds of soldiers and tradesmen of every kind to be catered for as well as thousands of prisoners. When the wars ended the captives were repatriated, the last of them leaving in February 1816. Princetown then went into decline from being a bustling township to the quiet wayside hamlet it had been to begin with.

The Plume of Feathers Inn – the first building in the town.

A rare photo of Princetown from the late 1800s. The building behind the horse and cart was the Policeman's house complete with cells. Photo courtesy of the late Clifford Waycott of Princetown.

A decorative frieze at Tor Royal depicting Tyrwhitt's tramway and trucks. Photo courtesy of Paul Rendell

The Duchy Hotel as it was before extensive renovation work in 1908. Note the moorstone (often called 'rubblestone' by estate agents) used in its construction 1806-1809.
Photo courtesy of the late Clifford Waycott of Princetown.

In an endeavour to promote further development a horse drawn tramway was opened in 1823 at the instigation of Sir Thomas Tyrwhitt. It connected Plymouth to the quarries on the western side of North Hessary and was later extended to the town itself, terminating at the rear of the Railway Inn in a walled off area known as The Wharf. Granite and some agricultural products were transported off the moor, the trains bringing back building materials, lime, and

The High Moorland Visitor Centre, formerly the Duchy Hotel and later the Prison Officers Mess.

sea-sand as a soil improver, but there was a lack of support and the line closed in 1869 by which time Sir Thomas had died (1833).

The prison stood empty until 1850 when it opened again, this time as a convict prison. Shortly afterwards the officers' accommodation was acquired by Mr. James Rowe who refurbished it before opening the 'Duchy Hotel'. It was an immediate success. The Prince Consort, Queen Victoria's husband Albert, was entertained there when he inspected the prison in 1852 (H.M. the Queen went to Plymouth that day and the sound of the guns firing a salute could be clearly heard in Princetown). Other notable guests included the Poet Laureate Alfred Lord Tennyson and doctor/author Sir Arthur Conan Doyle of Sherlock Holmes fame.

In 1908 further alterations were made to the hotel and its rough stone walls were rendered to the smooth exterior you see today (the words Duchy Hotel can still be seen at each end of the building). The extension to the right of the main entrance, constructed in a different style, was added in 1914 and the Duchy of Cornwall Office shares these premises. The title Duke of Cornwall has been invested in the Sovereign's eldest son since Edward the Black Prince was created the first Duke in 1337 and the Duchy Estates have provided an income for successive Dukes, much of it from large tracts of Dartmoor. The activities of the tinners, farmers, quarry owners, and so on attracted rents and taxes. Many of the properties in Princetown and the surrounding area are still leased from the Duchy – among them Dartmoor prison.

When Dartmoor ponies roamed the streets before cattle grids.

In 1941 'Duchy House' as it came to be called, was taken over by the prison for use as the Prison Officers Mess and for many years bachelor warders lived there. It was outside the 'Duchy' that Dartmoor prison's most notorious prisoner, Frank Mitchell the 'Mad Axeman', exhibited his enormous strength when passing by with a prison work party. A 'Triumph Vitesse' police car was parked outside with two officers in it. 'Big Frank' got a hold on the rear of the car, lifted it and turned it around 180 degrees, telling the occupants to proceed back to where they came from, but in not such polite terms!

In 1990 the Prison Officers Mess was transferred to the prison and the Dartmoor National Park Authority began converting this historic building into the present day Visitor Centre. It was officially opened by H.R.H. Prince Charles on 9 June 1993.

Between the Plume of Feathers Inn and the Railway Inn is an ancient track leading to the moor and a stunningly picturesque walk past Siwards Cross (commonly called 'Nuns Cross') to the ruins of Eylesbarrow Mine and southern Dartmoor. The path used to be known as 'Ivybridge Lane' and is still referred to by that name locally on account of it being used in the early days of the convict prison to escort convicts to and from the railway station at Ivybridge before the Plymouth to Tavistock line was built.

The house on the opposite side of the road with the inscription 'A.B. 1903' over the door was the home of Mr. Albert Bolt and his family who owned the adjoining shop and bakery. They sold everything a moorland family required at that time, including groceries, bread, dairy products, haberdashery, paraffin for Primus stoves, lamp oil, and coal. In the 1930s their two Ford vans were a familiar sight delivering these essential items to isolated farms and cottages, their drivers

Princetown's Railway Inn, once the terminus for Sir Thomas Tyrwhitt's tramway. Jubilee Lamp in the foreground.

A winter scene: clearing snow from the streets of Princetown, 1963.
Photo courtesy of the late Clifford Waycott of Princetown.

enduring the worst of Dartmoor weather to supply their customers with the necessities of life. Princetown's older inhabitants recall Miss Louie Bolt, a kindly soul who could never resist giving little gifts (usually sweets) to children. One of them, now an elderly lady, confessed to the author she and her friends often entered their store on a pretext, knowing they would be treated – and of course they always were! The Bolt family now rest in the churchyard and are remembered with affection.

A short distance along the Two Bridges road, by the Methodist Chapel, is a turning right which leads to the ruins of the tin mines at Whiteworks. These old mine workings are near Fox Tor Mire, a dangerous bog which featured as 'Grimpen Mire' in the famous Sherlock Holmes story 'The Hound of the Baskervilles'.

Albert Terrace and Two Bridges Road looking towards Plymouth Hill. An Edwardian glimpse of old Princetown. Mr Hooper's other drinking fountain at left of picture.
Photo courtesy of Mrs Rosie Oxenham.

Sir Thomas Tyrwhitt entertained his Regency friends at his Dartmoor home Tor Royal and farmed the estate he created there (it is still being farmed today). There were 'high jinks' there in Tyrwhitt's day, but there is no evidence to support the romantic notion that the Prince of Wales was ever a guest, despite the fact he and Sir Thomas were life-long friends. There is evidence of another tale though, the story of how a young man called Trebble fell in love with Dolly Copplestone, a local girl. Anxious to protect her from the attentions of the notorious 'Regency Rakes', he married her and installed her in a little cottage on the banks of the River Dart, to live in seclusion and safety. The ruins of 'Dolly's Cot' can still be seen in the woods at Dartmeet.

Tavistock Road from the Duchy Hotel forecourt, pre 1914. The extension which now houses the Duchy of Cornwall offices had not yet been built. Photo courtesy of Mrs Rosie Oxenham.

Dartmoor Prison and farm enclosures as they used to be.

Walk along Tavistock Road towards the prison. On a grassy area where Princetown Fair was held in days gone by is the War Memorial, and the end property next to it used to be the Police Station with cells for the detention of wrongdoers and a mortuary at the back. The local policeman lived here with his family. The most unusual prisoner to be confined here was ex-convict Joe Denny, a West Indian who broke *into* Dartmoor prison in November 1890 seeking revenge for having (allegedly) been badly treated during his eight months imprisonment there for felony. He was apprehended late at night inside the prison walls after attempting to set fire to the place and was handed over to the local Constable to be detained. He was later convicted and sentenced to twelve months hard labour for this and other offences.

Princetown County Primary School occupies the site of one of the two slaughterhouses (referred to as 'butcheries' at the time) where meat was prepared for the prisoners of war and the soldiers. Close by were two bakeries. If you stand to the left of the school and look out over the children's play area towards the moor you will notice fields enclosed by stone walls. This is prison land and the 'enclosures' as they are called, were reclaimed from the peat bogs by gangs of convicts who, during the late 1800s and early 1900s, broke up the ground by hand and drained it. The farmland they created robbed Princetown folk of their traditional peat diggings, their winter fuel supplies, and caused much hardship at that time.

Opposite the school beside the entrance to the 'Prince of Wales' is one of two drinking fountains erected in 1908 by R.H. Hooker, Esq. (the other one is in Two Bridges Road). They both have a lion's head from whose mouths spring water from the moor once flowed and both fountains have a small bronze tablet with the words: *'This fountain is erected in grateful acknowledgement of the*

Prince of Wales Inn and Mr Hooper's drinking fountain. Princetown Town Hall used to occupy the area to the right of the picture.

benefits received from the life giving air of Princetown'. If you are doubtful about this claim, have a look at the headstones in the churchyard – a large number of residents lived into their eighties and nineties and the first convicts at Dartmoor prison were invalids sent there for the benefit of their health.

Just a few steps away is the entrance to Station Road, a poignant reminder of Princetown's busier days when a branch line to Yelverton connected passengers to the Launceston – Tavistock – Plymouth railway, providing a link for families

Switching points. Princetown station signal box and station house in the background. Station cottages (left of signal box) mark the site today. Photo courtesy of the late Clifford Waycott of Princetown.

who wanted a day shopping, or perhaps sought entertainment in the city. Constructed and operated by the Great Western Railway, the line opened in 1883 and was very popular with ramblers and visitors to Princetown. Older Princetown inhabitants recall seeing convicts being escorted to Dartmoor on the 'Convict Express', as the train was light-heartedly called, and marching to the prison in chains.

The station itself, of which little trace remains, was the highest in England, but sadly it succumbed to the Age of the Car and closed in 1956. There can be no doubt had it stayed open just a little longer the line would have been a major attraction and a profitable one. The track bed, which follows the route of Sir Thomas Tyrwhitt's tramway for much of the way, has been preserved to provide an enjoyable walk of great scenic beauty.

Going towards the prison you pass a row of houses to your right named Hessary Terrace. This is one of several terraced properties in Princetown which were the homes of prison warders and their families whose terms of employment stipulated they had to live here. Today most prison officers commute from

The GWR railway line over Dartmoor. The train is approaching Princetown station after a tortuous uphill journey from Yelverton. From a painting by Paul Deacon.

Tavistock or Plymouth and many of the houses they once occupied are privately owned.

Note the house of modern design called 'Keystones', the last house on the left before you reach the church. This was the Police Station which was built in 1953 as a replacement (after nearly 100 years of service) for the older one previously referred to. The Princetown 'Bobby' had the largest beat in England – over 60,000 acres of moors and remote settlements. Unlike the conventional policeman, he performed his duties entirely unsupervised, with no fixed hours or routine and was often roused from his bed to deal with incidents perhaps many miles away. The Station was not only a workplace and dwelling, but a Command Centre for any trouble at the prison, including escapes. The resident Constable was always the first to be notified of an escape and subsequent developments were reported to him to forward to Police Headquarters by telephone (radio communication superseded this arrangement).

The house adjacent to the church is the Old Parsonage also built by the prisoners of war and now privately owned. It originally comprised three small cottages and a stable block. It was here a Frenchman devised a clever means of escape by persuading his comrades to entomb him in the chimney breast they were constructing. When they were marched back to the prison at the end of the day he was able to break free, the mortar not having yet fully set, and make his getaway.

Hessary Terrace. One of several terraces which were once the homes of Dartmoor Prison warders.

Opposite the Parsonage is Barrack Road and as the name indicates it was one of the main entrances to the barracks which housed the troops who guarded the prison. The barracks were pulled down after Dartmoor reopened as a convict prison and the grim grey building nearest the main road is all that is left of the several guardhouses. At the bottom of this road are two properties which represent the last remains of the barracks proper – Grosvenor House, now an apartment block and Dart Cottage.

The now redundant Prison Officers Ladies Club converted from one of the old barrack guard houses.

The Church and Churchyard.

The Parish Church of St Michael and All Angels, Princetown. An Edwardian picture taken when the church was at its best and before the Dartmoor weather took its toll.

The Parish Church of St. Michaels and All Angels is unique in England, having been constructed by the French and American prisoners of war (all volunteers and paid 6d. per day). From the main entrance the path takes you through the older part of the graveyard where prison warders of long ago share the parishioners last resting place. Turn right at the gate and make your way along the churchyard

The grave of Chief Warder George Palmer in Princetown churchyard

One of the convict headstones in the separate convict burial ground engraved with the dead man's initials and date of death only, as supplied by the prison.

wall to where a large stone, a hefty chunk of Dartmoor granite with a raised central brass memorial tablet, marks the grave of Chief Warder George Palmer who died in 1904. There is a story of how, as a young man, he often sat and rested on this stone whilst guarding convicts in the prison quarry and that his colleagues subscribed for and erected it in memory of a popular officer. To the left of the gate, below the stained glass window at the end of the church, you will find the grave and headstone of Capt. Oswald Every, the only prison Governor to have died in office. He succumbed to a bout of pneumonia in January 1892.

To the right and rear of the churchyard is the separate convict burial ground with rows of tiny headstones bearing the initials and date of death of prisoners who died after 1902. Before then they were interred in unmarked graves and the large plain granite cross by the church tower without an inscription is their only memorial. It was made and set up with convict labour in 1912. There are two prisoners' headstones separate from the others. One of them, identical to the rest, can be seen close to the large memorial cross just referred to. It is a Borstal Boy's grave and is inscribed simply '*R.G.P. 9-7-'46*' (a number of these young criminals were transferred to Dartmoor for a short while after World War Two). A traditional headstone stands in isolation in front of the other convict graves and is the only one to have been provided by a prisoner's family despite the fact they always had that right. The inscription reads: '*L.D.G. Died February 22nd. 1877. Aged 44 years. My Jesu Mercy.*'

Against the churchyard wall behind and to the right of the tower you will find the communal grave of 'Three Valiant Soldiers' who perished in a snowstorm in Feb. 1853. Two of them, both Privates, were marching from Dousland to report for duty when they were overwhelmed by the force of the storm. A Corporal was sent to look for them when they became overdue and also died. Their frozen bodies were later discovered on the Plymouth road not far from Princetown. They were: Corporal Joseph Penton aged 20, Private

The Three Valiant Soldiers headstone in Princetown churchyard

Patrick Carlin aged 23 and George Driver aged 27. They all served with the 7th. Royal Fusiliers doing guard duty at the prison. This road was also the route taken by the prisoners of war who were marched to Dartmoor Prison from Plymouth guarded by 'Redcoats'.

Inside the church is a memorial tablet in Italian marble to Sir Thomas Tyrwhitt. The inscription reads:

Sir Thomas Tyrwhitt, Knt.,

Late of Tor Royal, Lord Warden of the Stannaries,

And many years Usher of Black Rod,

Died Feb. 24th. 1833

Aged 71

'His name and memory are inseparable from all the Great Works on Dartmoor, and cannot cease to be Honoured in this District'

There is also a large stained glass memorial window (you can see it from the outside) donated by the United States Daughters of 1812, whose members are direct descendants of those who fought in that war. It bears the inscription:

To the Glory of God in Memory of the American Prisoners of War

who were detained in the Dartmoor War prison between the years

1809-1815 and who helped to build this church, especially of the 218* above men who died here on behalf of their Country.

'Dulce est Pro Patria Mori'.

*The true figure is now known to have been much higher – nearer 270.

Dartmoor weather has taken its toll however and the church had to close in 1994 having fallen into a state of disrepair through lack of funds. After 180 years the cold and frost and the wet finally rotted the floorboards, damaged the stonework, and rendered the tower unsafe. At the time of writing extensive repair work is under way sponsored by the Churches Conservation Trust, a body established by Parliament and the Church of England to preserve churches of historical or architectural interest, after which the church's future will have to be decided.

The memorial window in Princetown parish church dedicated to the American prisoners of war who were imprisoned at Dartmoor during the war of 1812 and of those who died there.

Dartmoor Prison

Leave the churchyard by the front gate and turn left. A short walk will bring you to the main entrance of one of the most famous prisons in the world. A huge granite arch stands before it through which marched prisoners of war and convicts of a later period. Inscribed over the arch are the words *'Parcere Subjectis' (Spare the Vanquished)*, an appropriate greeting for men taken in battle. Many of the buildings from the war depot days were demolished and rebuilt during the late

A view of the prison which shows the basic design, unchanged from when it was built (1806-1809). The main entrance with the famous arch is visible where the road at the bottom of the picture bears left.

1800s and early 1900s. Parts of the original war prison remain however – for example the Prison Officers Mess to the right of the arch where the 'Agents', as the first Governors were called, lived with their families. The circular boundary wall, roughly a mile in circumference, is the outer one of two walls which once

The work party leaving Dartmoor Prison main entrance under armed guards and swinging right almost certainly bound for the prison quarry (now redundant) c.1880.

1904 Convict work party man-hauling a prison cart.

enclosed the prison and the clump of trees at the rear of the establishment screens two cemeteries where the remains of over 1400 French and Americans are buried

Dartmoor Prison main entrance c.1880. The armed guards were responsible for security outside the prison walls and accompanied all outside work parties. Several convicts were shot, sometimes with fatal results while trying to run away. Working 'under the gun' finally ceased in 1954.
Photo courtesy of the late Clifford Waycott of Princetown.

in separate mass graves. A deadly type of measles and a smallpox epidemic killed the majority of them.

Opposite the arch, on the other side of the road behind the granite wall, is the reservoir and water control tower dating from the time the prison was built. The reservoir was supplied by a four mile long prison leat (shallow waterway) which extracted water from the River Walkham. This was supplemented in the convict days by spring water pumped from collecting points on Great Mis Tor. Treated 'bog water' as it was called was the

Dartmoor Prison Museum Curator, Brett Johnson and assistant Hazel Smith. The museum enables the visitor to look at prison life from the grim days of the prisoner of war depot to the present.

convict's lot until 1995 when South West Water installed a mains supply and rendered the leat redundant.

In Victorian times visitors to Princetown congregated to see the work parties march off to the fields and quarries accompanied by the Civil Guard armed with carbines and fixed bayonets. In those days Dartmoor held the 'tough men' from the prisons, all of whom had not less than five years to serve. Today the inmates are Category 'C' men (low risk prisoners) and among those in charge of them are a number of women officers who perform exactly the same duties as their male counterparts.

Much of the prison's history lies within Dartmoor Prison Museum just a few steps further towards Rundlestone. It occupies part of the prison itself, the Old Dairy, and houses a collection of historic artifacts associated with Dartmoor's past. It was from one of the toilets in this building that inmate 'Foxy' Fowler escaped one foggy day in 1957. They had recently been installed and the windows had not been adequately barred, presenting the 'Fox' with a rare opportunity. Despite being pursued by prison officers, police and a local hunt who abandoned their bushy-tailed quarry for a chase of another kind (hence the 'Foxy' label), he managed to elude them for 33 days before being recognised and apprehended in Cumberland more than 300 miles away.

'A Midnight Adventure'

Retracing your steps towards the town you will see, on the corner adjacent to the churchyard, a large granite built house with a walled garden. In the convict days this was the Chaplain's House. In the winter of 1895 the occupant, Rev. Clifford Rickards, B.A., experienced what he later termed a 'midnight adventure' when he disturbed a burglar late at night. When challenged, the intruder threatened him with a knife and a fierce struggle ensued during which the Reverend, who was a sporting man, managed to break free and despite severe gashes to his hands was able to grab his shotgun and load it. The burglar's mistake was in thinking a 'man of the cloth' would never shoot, but when threatened again with the knife he did just that, aiming at the hand raised against him. As a result a badly wounded criminal (he was afterwards imprisoned for this and other offences) was handed over to the local policeman who took him to Tavistock hospital where it was found necessary to amputate his arm. A contrite villain later told his intended victim he deserved all he got.

On your return to the town centre, just before you reach the 'Prince of Wales' inn, note the single storey accommodation for the elderly which stands on the site of Princetown's Town Hall (demolished in 1988). The hall was converted for use as a courtroom in the wake of the Dartmoor prison mutiny in January 1932 when nearly 200 convicts rioted, assaulted and injured several warders and destroyed the administration block and Governor's office by fire. Plymouth City police restored order, with an armed party of soldiers from Crownhill Barracks (Plymouth) standing by at the scene. The ringleaders were dealt with at a Special Assize set up in Princetown to save the expense and extra security needed to take them to Tavistock or Exeter. The Judge and Barristers used school classrooms to change into their robes and wigs. It was snowing heavily as they crossed the road and the roar of hailstones caused the proceedings to be halted on two occasions. The date was 9th. May 1932. Such is Dartmoor weather and if you have chosen a cold and dreary day to visit, then you will return with some idea of what was endured by the prisoners of war and the convicts of long ago.

1932. The aftermath of the mutiny during which rioting convicts set fire to the Administration building and clock tower. The picture shows the extent of the damage which destroyed the Governor's office and prison records.
Photo courtesy of P.C. Simon Dell, MBE of Tavistock

1932. Princetown Town hall (extreme left) where the ringleaders of the prison mutiny were tried at a Special Assize. Police and warders are about to escort the accused from the transport lorry into the building where a specially constructed dock awaited them.
Photo courtesy of P.C. Simon Dell, MBE of Tavistock

The Surrounding Area

For visitors who wish to explore further there are four main areas worthy of attention.

The Ockery and Two Bridges.

Leave Princetown by turning left at the mini-roundabout by the Visitor Centre. After passing the last houses and the lay-by (right) a dramatic view of the prison presents itself before the road descends to the Blackabrook river. The Devonport leat passes under the road half way down the hill. Originally over twenty miles long, it was constructed between 1793 and 1798 to supplement the water supply to Dock (now Devonport) and ships of the Royal Navy. It extracts water from three Dartmoor rivers: the East Dart, the Cowsic and the Blackabrook. Following the contours of hills and tors the combined contents flow by a tortuous route to join the River Meavy which in turn enters Burrator reservoir, the main water

The Ockery in times gone by. The clapper bridge is to the left of the road bridge behind the barn (which is still there). Only the foundations of the cottage remain today. The line of the Devonport Leat can be seen half way up the slope towards Princetown. Photo courtesy of Paul Rendell

Prison Quarry entrance 1880. The convicts are manhandling a cartload of stone, probably for building the prisons which replaced the old French prison blocks. Note the armed guards on the skyline.

supply for the Plymouth area. The road crosses the river adjacent to a clapper bridge ('clapper' - a simple structure of granite slabs supported on stone plinths). This little dell is known as the 'Ockery' (pronounced 'Oakery'). During the Napoleonic War and for more than 100 years afterwards a quaint cottage of unusual design stood above the tumbling waters. It is believed to have been built by Sir Thomas Tyrwhitt to house a miller and his family and was called simply Ockery Cottage, but local people referred to it as the 'French Commandant's House' (some of them still do) because according to tradition, two French Generals lived here for a time. Many French and American officers lived as free men 'on parole' in various towns around the moor, but Princetown was not one of these places. However, many a legend is based on fact and who knows what conditions prevailed at the time, unrecorded perhaps but stamped in the memories of successive generations of Princetown families. At the top of the hill a panoramic view of Two Bridges and the East Dart River valley is revealed. Crockern Tor, the meeting place of the ancient tinners, lies beyond on the Moreton road as do the Powder Mills where there was once a gunpowder factory.

'Redcoats' escorting French prisoners of war to Dartmoor. The stretcher and reclining prisoner bottom left suggest they were survivors from the Battle of Waterloo, over 14,000 of whom were confined on the 'moor'. From a painting by an unknown Dartmoor Prison inmate.

Rundlestone and Merrivale.
Proceed along Tavistock road past the prison entrance. The prison farm is on your right. More than once in the past when Princetown was cut off by snow, farm animals were killed and extra prison bread was baked to feed the town's residents as well as the jail's inmates. A short distance further, on a bend, you pass the entrance to the now disused prison quarry where convicts were subjected

to heartbreaking labour and where several men were killed in accidents. Near the Rundlestone road junction tents were erected in 1891 to enable victims of a cholera outbreak to be quarantined. The road left to Tavistock then passes the old tin workings (left) called Wheal Lucky and the redundant Mis Tor water pumping station just before a small parking area (left) from where a track leads to Yellowmead Farm and the now disused Foggintor, Swell Tor and King Tor quarries. Granite from this area was used for Nelson's Column in London, parts of the Houses of Parliament and replacement corbels (supports) for the Old London Bridge (in the 1960s it was sold to a wealthy American who dismantled it and flew the parts to Arizona where it was rebuilt as a very successful tourist attraction). More than 600 men were employed here up to the mid 1800s after which the quarries began to decline, unable to compete with the Cornish ones because of their remote location and transport costs. The last of them closed in 1938, but minor workings survived until as recently as 1966. Many workers and their families lived in cottages (now in ruins) situated along the track which runs towards the now abandoned workings. A little further towards Tavistock the main road passes a car park (left) known as 'Four Winds' and the ruined walls are all that is left of Foggintor School which the quarry worker's children attended. The school closed in 1936. Dartmoor boasts more prehistoric remains than anywhere else in Europe and a fine example of a stone row, together with a scattering of hut circles, can be seen to your left on the downhill approach to the once industrious Merrivale Quarry and thence to the old market town of Tavistock.

Princetown to Yelverton.

Turn right at the Visitor Centre and go up Plymouth Hill on the Yelverton road. Close by the cattle grid on the outskirts of Princetown you pass an area below Hessary Tor where in 1853 William Babb worked a clay pit for making bricks. His employees were housed in cottages he had built for them and their families which were known as Babbs Cottages. It was near here the Valiant Soldiers Corporal perished so close to safety. The bodies of the other two men were found further on. Going downhill from the outskirts of Princetown the track of the old GWR railway can be seen (right) and Station Cottages still mark the site of the station. Groups of French and American prisoners, hundreds strong and heavily guarded, tramped along this road from Plymouth and retraced their steps years later laughing and cheering on their way to be shipped home. Later still horse drawn wagons, contracted at Plymouth, transported convicts to Dartmoor before the advent of the railways (there was often an overnight stop at Dousland when the passengers assisted in unharnessing the horses and apparently made no attempt to escape). Some of the most outstanding views of Dartmoor and the border country are to be seen before reaching the cattle grid which marks the exit from the moor, including Sharpitor where an R.A.F. radio mast was a prominent landmark during and after World War 2. Black Tor was the scene of yet another winter tragedy when a rambler collapsed among the rocks from exhaustion. His friend made it to Princetown for help but his companion died of cold before they got to him.

Whiteworks and Peat Cott.

Turn into the road by the Methodist Chapel and proceed up the hill and down the other side. Where the road bears right you will catch sight of Tor Royal among the trees. A little further on Peat Cott is visible to your left. It was the home of the Worth family for several generations and this is how it came about: One day in the early 1800s a young man called Worth was using a scythe to cut hay in a nearby field and had forgotten to bring his sharpening stone. He knocked at the door of local baker Mr. Richard Edwards and was greeted by Charlotte, one of his four daughters. He borrowed a stone and duly returned it, but a love story was to follow with Mr. Worth developing a constant memory loss which entailed repeated knocking on that particular door! They were eventually married and the couple went to live at Peat Cott in a farmhouse they built themselves on the open moor (this story was related by the late Mrs.B. Cole, a great granddaughter of one of Charlotte's sisters). Charlotte Worth was a well known figure in Princetown and is remembered now as the 'Mother of Peat Cott'. She lived to be over 94 years of age and her father, who supplied bread to the French and Americans in the war prison, died in 1876 aged 99 – further testimony of the life giving air on Dartmoor! Her descendants lived there for generations and built a Methodist chapel complete with harmonium which neighbours from the Whiteworks tin mines and the surrounding area regularly attended. The road terminates at Whiteworks where the extensive ruins of the mines lie close to the Devonport leat. It bustled with activity at its peak in 1875 but like so many endeavours on Dartmoor the prosperity it brought was short-lived and it is a wild lonely spot today. Fox Tor mires are best avoided unless you have a guide.

Summary

Princetown's fortunes have fluctuated widely since the Napoleonic War. In 1813 the population was at its zenith with nearly 10,000 captives in the prison and 1200 military personnel. Add to this the prison administration and medical staff (some with families), various tradesmen, quarrymen and miners and it can be seen how the town then was truly the 'Capital of the Moor'. The population fell dramatically at the end of hostilities when the prisoners were sent home and the soldiers and tradesmen left, leaving Princetown a sad forgotten place inhabited by a few labourers and tradesmen. When Dartmoor Prison reopened in 1850 there was another revival with the influx of soldier guards and warders with families. Shops opened, the inns prospered, a recreation room and a school were established, giving birth to a new community quartered in newly-built government houses. Thirty years later the many hundreds of men employed in the still expanding mines and quarries were joined by gangs of navvies employed building the railway line and a second policeman was despatched to live there to assist in keeping the peace. By 1883 the navvies' work was done and the first steam train from Yelverton chuffed up the steep gradients to the little town, creating a welcome connection to the outside world and bringing the first of many visitors. However, by the 1960s the mines and quarries had long since closed (except for the Merrivale workings) and the last train had travelled the grand old railway. Most prison officers and their families vacated their homes about this time to live elsewhere, no longer being obliged to reside in Princetown, whose future once again looked bleak.

Now the town is growing again. Old properties are being renovated and sold for private occupation, former warders' homes are occupied by a mixture of council tenants and home buyers and a spirit of optimism prevails as a result of the several tourist initiatives sponsored by the National Park Authority. The everlasting beauty of the moor and a growing awareness of its past, together with a continuing fascination with Britain's most controversial jail, will ensure Princetown's future and prosperity.

SIGNIFICANT DATES

1337 Edward the Black Prince created Duke of Cornwall.

1772 Road from Tavistock to Moretonhampstead built and attracts improvers to Dartmoor.

1785 Thomas (later to be Sir Thomas) Tyrwhitt joins improvers on Dartmoor and builds Tor Royal.

1798 Devonport leat supplies water to Dock and the Royal Navy.

1809 First French prisoners of war transferred from Plymouth hulks. Military officers lodged in what is now the Visitors Centre. Soldiers in the barracks.

1812 War commences with America. Thomas Tyrwhitt Knighted and appointed Usher of Black Rod.

1813 American prisoners of war join the French in Dartmoor prison.

1814 Princetown Parish Church first service held in January. Building work still going on.

1816 Prison closes. Princetown in decline.

1823 Horse drawn tramway connects Foggintor quarries to Plymouth – later extended to Railway Inn.

1833 Sir Thomas dies at Calais. Unmarried.

1850 Dartmoor prison opens for convict prisoners. Transportation coming to an end.

1853 Three Valiant Soldiers and schoolteacher Sweeney die in snowstorms.

1883 Steam railway opens connecting Princetown to Plymouth.

1891 Cholera outbreak – tents erected at Rundlestone to quarantine victims.

1917 Convicts moved out and 1,000 'Conscientious Objectors' sent to Dartmoor prison, now designated a Government work camp.

1932 Prison mutiny. Prison records destroyed by fire. Special Assize at Princetown for ringleaders.

1951 Dartmoor National Park created.

1954 Prison warders disarmed. No more work 'under the gun'.

1956 Railway closed.

1993 High Moorland Visitors Centre opened by Prince Charles.

2001 Dartmoor prison regraded to Category 'C' (low risk inmates).